Journaling:
This is my life

501 Journal Prompts to Inspire Creativity and Passion

Emilee Day

Contents

Introduction

"Do you wait for things to happen, or do you make them happen yourself? I believe in writing your own story."

—Charlotte Eriksson

Your life doesn't always go as you want it to.

You trained every possible moment and put your heart and soul into practicing, but at the last go-round, you were cut from the basketball team.

You planned your university course calendar right down to the last credit and now they are telling you that there are not enough students registered for one of your crucial courses and you will have to take an elective instead.

Your boyfriend or girlfriend just sent you a text saying they have decided it will work best if you both start to see other people. That night you run into them at a party with your (former) best friend.

Growing up and getting a life of your own is hard to do, and days when disappointments happen remind you of that. Life is always throwing us curves, but none more harshly than in our teen and young adult years when we are still honing our coping skills.

My own adolescence had its challenges too, and that's what prompted me to write this book that I believe will help you through this time of your life.

My mom was in the military when I was growing up and my dad was a computer guru of sorts. The upshot of this mixture of professions was that we moved a great deal.

Unlike some of my friends who found it traumatic to move from one community to another, I had to absorb whole new countries and cultures, and sometimes with no more than a few weeks to prepare.

I would make friends and leave friends. I would get involved in sports teams and school activities and then abandon them. I was always the "new kid" trying to figure out the social cliques and power structures in every classroom.

These circumstances could have created a very difficult childhood, but oddly enough, I found it pretty ordinary in many ways. Our home life was stable despite being mobile and by the time I was a teenager, I accepted that I had a taste for adventure and for figuring out new places and people.

Perhaps I was just laying the groundwork for the profession I ultimately chose: psychology.

Or perhaps it was my secret weapon that kept me sane and relatively calm about life.

I kept a journal which I wrote in at least four times a week ever since I was seven years old. There was no subject too big or too small to get my pen started as it moved across the page.

I recorded all my experiences, my failures and successes alike, my friendships and romances and my broken hearts and jumbled feelings. I wrote about the pain of loss and the excitement of discovery. I wondered in my writing who I really was and what would become of me in life.

My journal was my closest confidante all through high school and college. This small routine of preparing myself for bed each night and then writing for two to 10 minutes somehow purged my mind and then I could sleep, regardless of what was troubling me.

At times I was kind and optimistic, at others I was hateful and full of despair. The pages never judged me or told me to snap out of it or that there were plenty of other fish in the sea.

When I had no idea what to do, my mind just let the words flow and somewhere, after many had left my head and landed on the page, they suddenly made sense and I could see the course I should take.

These words helped me ponder and eventually decide what I wanted to do with my life and whether or not a romantic relationship was working or needed to be discarded.

After I studied about the impact of journaling on teenagers and young adults, I became much more aware of the real significance of those written accounts of my life and how greatly they were contributing to my mental and physical health.

There are a number of scientific studies I will include in this book that show that keeping a journal can literally change your life.

Your daily writing habit will help you:

- Feel better about yourself during years of self-doubt and uncertainty about who you really are and how you relate to the world around you.

- Gain a more positive perspective on life by developing an awareness of events that are happening to you.

- Give you a place to air your deepest responses to the experiences and people you encounter, and in the process, lift the burden from your mind.

To me, writing in a journal is a kind of secret weapon to deal with whatever life throws at you.

This book is geared especially to readers in their young adulthood and teen years because of all the periods of discovery in life, those years are the most amazing and in need of the most understanding.

Your daily words will help you understand the big questions of your life, like "who am I and what am I going to do with my life?"

They help you figure out the boundaries of friendship and love, and learn to deal with betrayal and trust and success and failure.

When you write in your journal, your words are not judged or misunderstood or twisted and thrown back at you. Your words are for you only, and you take careful steps to keep it that way.

Being a confirmed journal-writer myself inspired me to write this book for you because I believe it can make a world of difference in your life.

In the pages that follow, I will describe the science that supports what I am saying. I will teach you how to get started journaling, how to overcome roadblocks and stick with your daily writing as a good habit.

I will talk about the kinds of things that can go into a journal and the different kinds of journals, and whether or not you want to write it by hand or type it into an Internet journal.

To ensure that you have all the information you need to begin your journaling, this book is being written in three sections:

Part One is where we talk about what journaling is, why it is a good idea, how to get started, how to organize your journal entries in case you need to refer back to them (and that's rather fun in its own way) and how to maintain the habit of writing about your life.

Part Two is your ultimate guide to getting started. It consists of 501 writing prompts to help make journal writing fun and reflective.

Part Three offers more inspiration with 25 additional ideas for journaling, complete with different ideas of how this could work for you. As you will see, there is no "one size fits all" when it comes to finding your unique journaling style.

PART ONE

CHAPTER 1

Why You Should Start Journaling Now

"Once you start recognizing the truth of your story, finish the story. It happened but you're still here, you're still capable, powerful, you're not your circumstance. It happened and you made it through. You're still fully equipped with every single tool you need to fulfill your purpose."

– Steve Maraboli

As she tours the world, Lady Gaga writes down her thoughts and observations about her day in her journal.

It has what she feels or believes about what she sees, sketches, pictures and even letters between herself and her mother, Cynthia. Each trip brings a new journal. She keeps them all together and told a source once that if she ever has children, they'll be able to read all about their pop star mom, not just what made the headlines. She has hinted that someday she might even let them be published, but certainly not now.

She is not the only famous person who makes personal journaling a part of coping with the stresses and upheavals of everyday life. Actresses Jessica Simpson and Jennifer Aniston are both confirmed journal-keepers.

Jessica uses her journals as a therapeutic aide to unload her emotions. Her books contain a lot of stories about heartbreak and perseverance. She often goes back and rereads her journal to get inspiration for her songs.

Jennifer Aniston has been writing in a journal since she was 13 and refers to her books as her therapy sessions. She purchases simple leather diaries and once filled, she locks them safely away in her home.

They chronicle her boyfriends and the nature of her relationships, her friendships, her work and her family.

Unburdening herself in private allows her to not lose control in public, she says.

Now science is showing that if you journal like Lady Gaga and Jessica and Jennifer, you are well on your way to ensuring your good mental health.

Apparently, keeping too much personal information and trauma about your experiences stored in your head can cause a conflict between the two regions of your brain, and that leads to a reduction in your cognitive function, or your ability to think clearly.

Suppose that you have engaged in a behavior that you know would conflict with your parents or teachers, or you witness a friend engaged in it. You know you have to keep quiet about it. If you talk, you will either get yourself or your friend into trouble, and you don't want to do either. The secret becomes a little burden in your head.

But Dr. David Eagleman, a neuroscientist at Baylor College of Medicine and author of the book *Incognito: The Secret Lives of the Brain,* has determined that the simple act of jotting down a secret that troubles you may undo the harm of your stress about what has happened. In other words, a journal is a healing tool.

Dr. Eagleman writes that keeping secrets bottled up inside of you is bad for your brain. It results in a rivalry of brain parts fighting inside of your head.

One region of your brain wants to unload the information to relieve the stress it is causing and the other wants to bury it deep in your subconscious. One region will ultimately be the victor, but in the meantime, all that brain fighting will exhaust you and make you unable to deal with other things.

Psychologist Dr. Clayton Critcher, researcher at the University of California, Berkeley, casts more light on what happens when we try to keep things quiet in our heads.

His study, published in the *Journal of Experimental Psychology,* determined that when we keep secrets it takes so much energy and our brain becomes too exhausted to do other tasks. He tested students about the nature of their sexuality, for example, and discovered when they had to conceal their true sexuality, they were physically weaker and more easily angered than those who did not have to hide their sexuality.

But what you are concealing is still a secret, so you are not free to tell the first person who asks. So you need to unload it somehow, and that is where journaling comes into play.

Lucia Capacchione, author of *The Well-Being Journal,* says the perfect vehicle for unloading is your journal. She noted that the non-judgmental aspect of a journal is vitally important in the process.

She suggests that journaling is especially helpful for teens and young adults when you are dealing with such difficult times as having to move away from your family or friends, when your parents are divorcing or separating, school classes, your illness or a family member's injury, grade changes, deaths, births and fights with others.

When bad stuff happens, you naturally feel hurt and stressed and sometimes confused, insecure, angry, sad, fearful or grief-stricken. You need to talk about the situation, and sometimes you need that very special kind of friend that does not judge and does not talk back: your journal.

While the traditional way to keep a journal is to use words it is not the only way, as Part Three of this book will show. You may want to draw out your feelings or just write freestyle with no sentences or paragraphs or punctuation to slow you down.

Sometimes the act of writing about the situation can bring you relief or a solution. One researcher who has done a lot of work in determining the impact of writing in a journal on mental health is Dr. James Pennebaker, a psychologist at the University of Texas at Austin. He has suggested that just the process of writing down your trauma helps to unclog your brain.

He proved this by using electroencephalography, a special tool that measures brain waves, on students to see how their brain was impacted when they divulged a trauma they had been keeping a secret. He discovered that letting go of the trauma through writing allowed the left and right sides of the brain to communicate with each other again.

In other studies, psychologist Dr. Pennebaker showed how writing about our secrets and deepest concerns can decrease the level of stress hormones in our bodies and even heighten our immune system and make us less apt to become sick.

He also found that writing regularly in your journal can improve your working memory, help you reduce mistakes at work or in the classroom, and help you cope better with stressful situations in the future.

If you are convinced of the benefits of journal writing now, but are still not sure how you can get started and fit it into your already busy life, you will learn how in the next chapter.

CHAPTER 2

How to Get Started

"The journal is a vehicle for my sense of selfhood. It represents me as emotionally and spiritually independent. Therefore (alas) it does not simply record my actual, daily life but rather – in many cases – offers an alternative to it."

– Susan Sontag

Ryan Gosling required actors in *Lost River* to keep a dream journal as he entered into the director's role for the first time. He believed that it would help all of them to better connect with the material they were working with.

The 34-year actor said they weren't all in favor of the idea at the start, but when they began to see how well it was working, they became more excited and committed to the process.

Gosling explained that the journals played into the overall theme of the movie, which was about a woman whose dream was turning into a nightmare. The director thought the actors, by keeping their own dream journals, could explore the idea privately and literally.

This is a practical example of how the experience of journaling can influence our creativity and development.

You will find that you will get some interesting results as well when you start your own journaling experience.

When you begin to write entries in your journal, it is not unusual to pour out negative thoughts. One of the first things that you will notice is that suddenly you feel better.

A study published in the journal *Psychological Science* gives insight into why you feel as you do. According to psychologist Dr. Richard Petty of Ohio State University, the process of writing to feel better really works. He suggests that by physically throwing out your thoughts onto the page, you are suddenly able to take control of them.

In the same way, keeping a gratitude journal can help you to feel happier, and writing about stress can reduce it.

So how do you get started?

An excellent technique is to just sit down with your journal and start to write freestyle, with no plot or plan and no special attention to spelling or sentences or even punctuation. Just let your thoughts flow and come unbidden to your head. Let your subconscious mind take over and start writing automatically. It doesn't have to make sense; this is not an English test or an assigned composition. It is just an outpouring of what is in your brain.

If free writing isn't your style, you could also start your journal by writing a few bullet points. Jot down four of five things that are interesting to you that day. It can be any subject or a full range of subjects. Just taking a short and simple approach to journaling is another way to get started.

It's also a good idea to try journaling at different times throughout your first week and see what time works best to begin your new habit. You will find a pattern evolves. Some people like to enter items in their journal at the start of the day, perhaps during breakfast, and others stop to recollect their day when they return home after class or after work. The bulk of habitual journal-writers make it part of their bedtime routine, taking a few minutes late in the evening to recount their day and rid their mind of their worry.

You will find as you get going that there are other side effects to journaling. For one thing, you will find yourself being more observant. You may also find, over time, that the negative entries are soon overshadowed by positive entries about your goals and your plans.

You will also find it easier to express yourself and review the highlights of your days, your weeks and your months. You will see the progress of your thinking over time, and how you develop coping skills.

Remember in your early days of journaling that no one but you will read what you write, so you don't have to spend any time worrying about making it perfect. You just have to allow what is in your brain and heart to pour out onto the page.

In a blog post called "Keeping a Journal to Enhance Your Life & The World," Ali Luke summed up the personal impact blogging had on her life. She said that we learn about the world outside us by reading, but we learn about the world inside us by writing.

It is through the daily stories of your life that you will soon be able to see patterns emerge, to identify things that obsess you, and resolutions that you constantly make and break. As you get to know yourself better, you begin to change and grow and your true self emerges.

CHAPTER 3

How to Overcome Roadblocks in Your Journaling Habit

"Isn't it mysterious to begin a new journal like this? I can run my fingers through the fresh clean pages but I cannot guess what the writing on them will be."
—Maud Hart Lovelace, Betsy in Spite of Herself

Journaling is like any other habit. If you expect it to stay a part of your routine, you have to ensure that you set aside time in the beginning and do not ever go more than two days without putting an entry in your journal.

I missed three weeks once during final exams followed by recovery time, and when I started to recount all the things that had happened in those 21 days, I could not remember nearly as much as I thought I would.

If your life follows a basic routine, it is not difficult to make journaling fit into it. The problem arises if your schedule suddenly changes, or you have company, or someone close to you or yourself gets ill, then everything changes and it can get lost in the chaos.

Ironically, those are the times when you most need it.

As a general standard, your memory will hold 48 hours of activities and thoughts and ideas, but after that they start to slip away and it gets harder and harder to capture your thoughts about things that are important to you.

A good way to establish the habit of journaling is to combine it with other things that you know you will rarely forget to do on any given day. For example, if it is your intention to write in your journal every evening, do it just after you brush your teeth for the night. The second habit is so engrained that it will be much easier to trigger the new habit.

If you normally write in the morning, link it to a process of your wake-up routine. If you normally write at the end of your classes or work, then link it to something else that you usually do as you arrive home, such as change into more comfortable clothing or grab a quick snack.

Be sure to always keep your journal in the same place so you can grab it in a second and get started. I keep my journal hidden in almost plain site under a box of tissues on the top of my bureau. I also always keep a pen right beside it.

From the beginning, I decided to use journals with nicely-designed hard covers because I find them very appealing. You may prefer the discreteness of moleskin or something larger and flashier; it doesn't matter.

It does make sense to stick with a particular size for your journals so you can store them easily over time.

What is amazing about the whole process of chronicling your day is how quickly a mass of impressions, ideas, observations and thoughts gather and begin to fill your first book.

You cannot begin to anticipate when you begin to write about your life each day how your life is going to evolve. Who knows? While the bulk of what you write will always be secret, you may someday become famous and decide to write your life story. Think how much easier this would be if you have a series of journals that guide you over all the key parts of your life.

Diaries and journals of our ancestors are useful now as well to give us insight into how our world has changed over the years. Depending on how intimate your journal is, you may also find it will someday fascinate your children or grandchildren to get a rare and personal view of what the world was like decades ago.

It is worth mentioning these things, but it is also vital to remember that you will gain the most therapeutic value from keeping your journal if you always write as if nobody will ever read it. Just as we are encouraged to dance as if nobody is watching or sing as if no one can hear, so too should write like nobody will read it.

There is a tremendous freedom that comes with that, and in that process of pouring out what comes to you instinctively, your real personal development will grow stronger.

CHAPTER 4

What Happens if You Lose Your Journal?

"Advice to Young Journal Keepers. Be lenient with yourself. Conceal your worst faults, leave out your most shameful thoughts, actions, and temptations. Give yourself all the good and interesting qualities you want and haven't got. If you should die young, what comfort would it be to your relatives to read the truth and have to say: It is not a pearl we have lost, but a swine?"

— Rosamond Lehmann, Invitation to the Waltz

The most frightening thing about keeping a journal for most people is that they might lose it, or that it might be read by someone else. If you live at home with your parents and siblings, that fear is magnified.

At the same time, you know that the full benefits of journaling are only experienced when you write freely and without fear of reprisals. Yet the possibility that someone might ultimately see your words can seriously inhibit your expression.

What's to be done about the whole privacy issue with your journal?

There are some obvious steps you can take to protect yourself, starting with keeping your journal in a private place and perhaps purchasing a type of journal that has a lock. You might also just want to keep it in a locked box underneath a shoebox or sweater box in your closet.

But there are other things you can do to protect your privacy. If you are angry with someone close to you and wish to write unpleasant things about them (as in a parent, partner, sibling or best friend), consider writing those entries on separate sheets of paper rather than right in the journal you will be keeping.

Once you have solidified your thoughts about that person and the situation that has angered you, you can then tear up the sheets and throw them in the garbage. Many journal-writers also devise a code for certain people in their life.

Don't talk about your journaling habit with others because it makes it sound enticing and something to be sought out. This is one habit that is completely between you and the pages you write on. Never read portions of it to even your best friend or trusted brother or sister; it will make them curious about what else you have written about.

Stephanie Dowrick, author of *Creative Journal Writing: The Art and Heart of Reflection,* protected her journals by locking them away but in her will she left a note explaining them to her children. She wrote:

"For much of my life I have kept journals. These have been a sort of 'stress management' to help me deal with life's troubles. You are welcome to read these journals or destroy them – your choice. But if you do read them, you may be struck by the negativity, the honesty and the struggles. Please temper your reactions with compassion and empathy. There have been many bumps along the way for me, but I truly believe that whatever happened did so for a reason – these were lessons I needed to learn."

It's a wonderful sentiment. If you are hindered from self-expression because of a fear that someday another person will read your journal, you may ease that burden by simply writing that in the front of each new journal. Couple that with using codes for key people in your life and write with ease.

Keep in mind that you are less likely to ever lose a journal if you always keep them in the same place. Loss is more likely to occur if you like to move around and keep your journal with you. If you do that, inevitably you will misplace one. If you must keep them with you, if you are using codes and do not have your name anywhere in it, perhaps the person finding it won't know that it is yours. But that is a risk and overall it makes more sense to keep them safely at home.

If the worst happens, and a parent, sibling or friend finds your journal and confronts you about its contents, do not react with outrage, even though it may be upsetting for someone to invade your privacy to this extent.

Tell the person calmly that you feel violated by their intrusion into the most private part of your life. Explain that you use your journal as a kind of catharsis, a way of working through life and solving problems. It is not meant as your final word or opinion on any subject or person.

You may even suggest that they try journaling for themselves.

CHAPTER 5

Do You Prefer Handwriting Your Journal or Going Digital?

"These empty pages are your future, soon to become your past. They will read the most personal tale you shall ever find in a book."

— Anonymous

There are so many journals on the market today that you may find it a delight to select the ones that you like best. Even discount stores often have a bin of beautifully-covered journals that you can pick up for under $5, while luxury stores have leather-bound versions.

Some offer lined pages and some unlined. Some have rings so you can easily tear out a page and destroy it if you want to; others have pages tightly glued in place.

Select the style and size that works best for you, and in the early stages of your new habit allow yourself the freedom to try a few different kinds to determine what feels right to you as you sit down to write.

When purchasing paper journals, just make sure that the paper is heavy enough that your writing will not leak through to the next page. If you enjoy adding art done with markers or paints to your journal, you may want to use a sketchbook of heavier paper than the average journal. You can write in a scrapbook style journal as well, especially if you want to post photos in it.

I like to alter the color of ink I use in my journals sometimes just for variety's sake, but I have known other writers who have a favorite pen that they prefer to use exclusively for their journaling. Most journal-writers find the process more pleasant if they have a nice pen and paper; it simply adds to the richness of the experience.

Online journaling is another option as well. You may believe that because you do all your essays and other writing on a computer that you will be more comfortable using a keyboard, and that is possible. However, I urge you to try pen and paper first just to check out your theory. You may discover that the change works well for you.

But online journals also have advantages, most notably that they make it easier to organize your entries and easily search through your hashtags to pull out all your writings on a particular subject.

One of the longest-standing and best known of the online journals is www.penzu.com. Here you can find free online journals totally focused on privacy. The advantages are that it is available to you anywhere and is particularly useful if you travel a lot or move around quite a bit in your studies or your job.

You can design custom covers, backgrounds and fonts with this website.

For the really mobile, there is also a Penzu mobile app for your iPhone, iPad and Android phones and tablets.

Another free online journal can be found at www.my-diary.org. It also offers excellent security and the freedom to be able to search your entries and categorize things for future reference.

The only thing to avoid in journaling is deciding to do it as a blog. While it is fine to write about your life, for the true therapy of journaling and all its benefits, you must be able to write with the assurance that your words will stay private. Only then can you really express what is deeply troubling or find honesty in your impressions.

CHAPTER 6

How to Keep Up with Your Journaling Practice

"For any writer who wants to keep a journal, be alive to everything, not just to what you're feeling, but also to your pets, to flowers, to what you're reading."

— May Sarton

The more often you journal, the more skillful you will become at observing life, capturing your reactions to it, sorting out your impressions and unburdening your mind.

That is why it is so important to maintain your journaling practice once you start it.

If you do miss a few days, jog your memory about what happened by checking your agenda, emails, texts, social media, etc.

You will be more inclined to continue your new habit if you write in a comfortable setting where you are relaxed and quiet, free from being interrupted. Many people like to start their writing by first relaxing themselves and clearing their mind. They sit still for a moment, and then inhale and exhale deeply three times before they pick up their pen.

Others like to play quiet music in the background, or light a scented candle and write with the shadows of light flickering across their page.

As you become more engaged with writing about your day, you will develop little routines that enhance the experience. Embrace them, for this is the ultimate "me" time. You will find that some days you have only two minutes to jot down highlights in bullet point form, while other days you spend 30 minutes writing at length about a new situation you are trying to figure out.

Some people write lists of things as a way of getting started and others intersperse their words with drawings or doodles or even the occasional poem.

However you maintain your journal writing habit, know that writing about the ups and downs of your life will help you keep your perspective, which is not always easy to do in the fluctuating world of adolescence and young adulthood.

Do not worry if your impressions and opinions change from day to day as you work things out; that is a normal part of the process. In fact, the philosopher William James believed that "if you can change your mind, you can change your life", and there is no better way to grow your thoughts than through journal-keeping.

It is a way to remind yourself every day that you are the owner of your own story, and only you personally understand the depth of your feelings about the things that happen to you.

These are the years that you face many, many demands and must deal with the expectations of others. You have classes, after class activities, work and chores, family responsibilities to uphold, obligations to friends and sometimes you feel stretched very thin.

If you occasionally feel as if the real you is getting lost in your world, reconnecting with who you are and what you feel for a few minutes each day will help put things back in focus. You can analyze your day, consider your future, and for a few minutes be totally self-centered.

There is nothing wrong with that. In fact, everyone needs a little time to focus only on themselves in life; otherwise we can get lost in the crowd.

PART TWO

If you start keeping a journal today and the habit stays with you for a lifetime, you will amass quite a few notebooks over the years. If you have no way of organizing them, and yet you want to go back and reread an entry some years later, or read everything about one subject (and that can be a lot of fun to see how you change over the years), you need to find a way from the beginning to organize them.

One effective way is to group topics together just as you would tweets about the same subject. Create hashtags to identify all entries about certain subjects. That way, if you do go back after a few years to review all the movies that interested you over the years, for example, you can find them easily by looking for # Love.

To get you started, here are 500 writing prompts on a wide variety of subjects that many of us encounter in our daily lives. Any day that you are having trouble getting started, grab a prompt and get going!

Five Hundred Journal Writing Prompts

"It has always been on the written page that the world has come into focus for me. If I can piece all these bits of memory together with the diaries and letters and the scribbled thoughts that clutter my mind and bookshelves, then maybe I can explain what happened. Maybe the worlds I have inhabited for the past seven years will assume order and logic and wholeness on paper. Maybe I can tell my story in a way that is useful to someone else."

— Nancy Horan, Loving Frank

#Feelings

1. To really be in love would feel like …

2. Gratitude is happiness doubled by wonder. (Gilbert K. Chesterton) Here are five things that I feel really grateful for in my life:

3. Is it ever okay to say, even in the privacy of your journal, that you feel like you hate someone? I hope so because …

4. If people are given the chance to experience life in more than one country, they will hate a little less. (Marjane Strapi) Every time I travel to a new place I feel that people are all different and yet in many ways all the same. They …

5. It feels really good to laugh hard but it is not something I do every day. The last thing that made me crack up was …

6. I feel really sorry about ….

7. Every day something happens that makes me feel grateful. Today I had that feeling when …

8. Most days I feel like I am just going through the motions, but something happened today to make me think that my life could be really different. This is the incident that occurred:

9. Sometimes you just feel you are in a good place. That's how I felt when …

10. I think sometimes that I am too hard on myself. Is my judgment too harsh? Tomorrow I will forgive myself when …

11. I felt really proud when …

12. I feel happy when I …

13. Should something be relevant in your life to be worth the effort of learning it? That question comes up every time I

14. When I see other people suffering, it really upsets me. Perhaps I have too much empathy, but …

15. What does my home really mean to me? I think it …

16. My first day in a new classroom always makes me feel like …

17. The worst part-time job I ever had was …

18. The best thing that happened to me today was …

19.   I feel sad when ….

20.   I feel very excited to be able to ….

21.   When I am alone in my room I feel ….

22.   When I see a couple walking hand in hand, I feel …

23.   When I have to write an exam, I feel …

24.   The best form of transportation is….

25.   When I wake up with a sore throat I feel …

26.   There's something about Saturdays that makes me feel ….

#Fun

27.   Last night was quite possibly the best party I have ever attended. …

28.   I think my favorite place to have fun is …

29.   I think it is fun to give and get surprises. For example …

30.   The best event I ever attended was …

31.   I went horseback riding (or water skiing, or snorkeling, etc.) for the first time. It was …

32.   Who knew how much fun organizing a (plant sale, bake sale, marathon, etc.) could be? What started out as my charity work turned into an adventure that all of us would remember. We …

33.   I think doing something unexpected is sometimes fun. The last unplanned fun I had was when …

34.   When I have a day off, I like to …

35.   My favorite way to exercise is to …

36.   The one fun activity I could do over and over again is to …

37.   If I thought the world would end tomorrow, I would …

38.   Hanging out with friends makes me feel like …

39.   The silliest thing I enjoy doing is …

40.   What's fun about being a boy (girl) is that …

41.   Today the most thing I did that was fun thing was to …

#Self-knowledge is self-taught

42.   Turn your attention for a while away from the worries and anxieties. Remind yourself of all your many blessings. (Ralph Marston) What is it in my life that really works well for me personally?

43.   This is how I would describe myself. I am …

44.   I love life because what more is there? (Anthony Hopkins) Here are five things that make my life different from the lives of my friends:

45.   If a stranger met me at a party and then discussed me with others after I left, this is what I hope they would say…

46. How wonderful it is that nobody need wait a single moment before starting to improve the world. (Anne Frank) What one action could I take tomorrow that would change my world for the better?

47. I felt proud when I …

48. I think that nobody understands me because ….

49. My best quality is …

50. If I have one unique talent, it is to …

51. I feel the best about myself when I …

52. I am happy when I am …

53. My favorite story about myself is…

54. As a child, I was …

55. Here are five unusual things that have happened to me so far in life:

56. I feel calmest when I …

#Bestfriends

57. Blessed is the influence of one true, loving human soul on another. (George Eliot) My best friend is ….

58. My friends have a lot of influence on me. They influence how I …

59.   Sometimes when people are with their friends they find it hard to maintain their individuality. For me, I've found that …

60.   A true friend is the greatest of all blessings, and that which we take the least care of all to acquire. (Francois de La Rochefoucauld) I met the people I consider my friends in all kinds of different ways…

61.   Instead of comparing our lot with that of those who are more fortunate than we are, we should compare it with the lot of the great majority of our fellow men. It then appears that we are among the privileged. (Helen Keller) I have many friends who seem to have a lot more riches than I have. Why is their life so easy and mine is…

62.   I show that I am loyal to my friends by…

63.   Laughter is not at all a bad beginning for a friendship, and it is far the best ending for one. (Oscar Wilde) Here are three things my best friend and I laugh about:

64.   My friends support me by …

65.   There are untold joys awaiting you when you stop caring about what others think and start living the life you've been blessed with. (Anonymous) When I think about what others think about me, I …

66.   I feel weak when I …

67. Walking with a friend in the dark is better than walking alone in the light. (Helen Keller) There have been so many experiences I have enjoyed that I would have lacked the courage to do were it not for my friends. I remember when I …

68. I find it hard to make friends because …

69. Can anything hurt more than being betrayed by someone you thought was your friend?

70. My friends think I am crazy because I want to …

71. I like my friend…but I am tired of his/her attempts to control my life.

#Talking about the weather

72. I love a rainy day. It makes me want to …

73. Is there anything nicer than a hot, sunny day? This day was perfect in that regard, so I ….

74. The temperature affects many people. For me …

75. Look at the trees, look at the birds, look at the clouds, look at the stars…and if you have eyes you will be able to see that the whole of existence is joyful. (Osho) This is what I can see in my back yard …

76. A cloudy day or a little sunshine have as great an influence on many constitutions as the most recent blessings or misfortunes. (Joseph Addison) When it is ….

77. I feel a sense of renewal whenever …

78. Walk as if you are kissing the Earth with your feet.
     (Buddhist prayer) I spend a lot of my day walking and I enjoy
     it because …

79. I want to spend more time …

80. Nature's peace will flow into you as sunshine flows into trees.
     (John Muir) Adolescence and young adulthood is a time of
     great learning but also many troubles as we come to terms
     with life. When I am troubled, this is how I find peace of
     mind. I go outside and …

81. Every so often I feel a need to get close to nature. It always
     catches me by surprise, a sense that I must …

82. One generation goes and another generation comes; but the
     earth remains forever. (Ecclesiastes) I wonder what the world
     that my children will inherit will look like. Will it be safe for
     them to live, or will it be …

83. Tomorrow I am going to start to change the world by…

84. Life is broadened when you grow something that comes out
     of the soil. It is …

85. Earth provides enough to satisfy every man's need, but not
     every man's greed. (Mahatma Gandhi) Sometimes I wonder if
     I have too much "stuff" in my life. Do I really need …

86. In nature, I like to observe…

#The working life

87.   My boss is ...

88.   My colleagues at work are ...

89.   Here are three careers that don't interest me:

90.   My favorite work project was when ...

91.   The best compliment I received was that ...

92.   I had an unusual experience at work today ...

93.   Sometimes work is satisfying. For example ...

94.   I don't know how much longer I can stand my job. Today ...

95.   I have to say this: my boss is different. Today ...

96.   I am working to fit in with my colleagues by ...

97.   I now know the kind of work I want to spend my life doing. I want to ...

98.   My goal is to get through my work day without ...

99.   Here are three careers that I think are fascinating:

100. My favorite part-time job was when I ...

101. Today I met a person at work who really inspired me. He/she was ...

Music to my ears

102. Right now my favorite song is … I like it because …

103. I absolutely love …He/she is such a good musician because …

104. The classic song I like best is …

105. Music has a great impact on my life. I play it when …

106. Of all the instruments, I want to play the …

107. My parents don't understand the kind of music I enjoy. I wish …

108. Music makes me feel …

109. Music in the soul can be heard by the universe. (Lao Tzu) The last concert I attended was …

110. No matter how upset I get, if I can play my … I feel better. It makes me …

111. There is no feeling, except for the extremes of fear and grief, that does not find relief in music. (George Eliot) When I am worried about something, I like to listen to …

112. I wonder what it would be like to be Taylor Swift. Does she….

113. I would like to learn to play the …

114. I like to listen to music when I …

115. The person I would most like to see in a concert is ... because ...

116. If I had all the money in the world, I would hold a big party and invite ....to play for all my friends. I think they would be perfect because ...

#Food for the senses

117. My favorite fast food is ...

118. I focus my diet on ...

119. My favorite comfort food is ...

120. There's no better feeling in the world than a warm pizza box on your lap. – Kevin James. The best pizza in my neighborhood is made by ...

121. My favorite flavor of ice cream is ...

122. I want to lose some weight and I just don't know where to start. I'm overwhelmed by ...

123. If you can't feed a hundred people, then feed just one. (Mother Teresa) Today I volunteered at the local food bank and ...

124. My favorite food day is.... because that's when my friends and I get together to eat ...

125. If you really want to make a friend, go to someone's house and eat with him ... the people who give you their food give you their heart. (Cesar Chavez) You learn a lot when you go to a friend's house to eat. For example ...

126. I just got the recipe of the century. Here it is …

127. The most beautiful birthday cake I ever had was …

128. One of my favorite bakeries is … because …

129. The restaurant I most like to eat at is … because …

130. I want to make a romantic meal for … It should include …

#Freedom's many forms

131. The best road to progress is freedom's road. (John F. Kennedy) I am ready to make my own decisions now, but I feel held back by …

132. Is freedom anything else than the right to live as we wish? (Epictetus) I really want the freedom to make my own decisions in life. I am tired of …

133. When I am by myself, I like to …

134. Freedom is from within. (Frank Lloyd Wright) People can insist on rules and that I act a certain way, but nobody can control what I think deep inside of myself. I think that …

135. If I could be any animal, I would be a …

136. If I had complete freedom to live anywhere, I would live in …

137. If I were the president, I would …

138. I want the freedom to choose my own profession but that will not be easy for me because …

139. I love that line in an old Janis Joplin song that says "freedom's just another word for nothing left to lose." I think that is true because …

140. I am very tired of trying to live by everyone else's rules …

#Loving others and you

141. Do I love you because you're beautiful, or are you beautiful because I love you? (Richard Rodgers) This is what I think is particularly beautiful in the person I love:

142. It's often just enough to be with someone. (Marilyn Monroe) When I am with … I feel that my world is full. Just spending time together makes me feel …

143. When I make love with …, it makes me feel ….

144. The most memorable kiss I have experienced so far in life was when …

145. There are so many kinds of love in my life …

146. It hurts unbearably to find out that your lover is cheating on you. I am …

147. The first time I walked hand in hand with …. in public it felt …

148. Hearing the words "I love you" has made me feel …

149. I never thought I would really fall irrationally in love, but …

150. What is it that makes us fall for those who are bad for us? Could it be …

151. I am totally in love and it is unlike anything I could have imagined. It feels …

152. I should have seen the signs that things were going wrong between us. For example …

153. Here it is; another Valentine's Day and I do not have anyone special in my life. I am …

154. Some people say there is a difference between having sex and making love. For me the difference is …

155. What would my perfect partner be like? They would …

156. I hate being lied to, especially by someone who professes to care about me …

157. #Health and wellness

158. Every day I try to do one thing that is good for me. Today I …

159. When I feel sick physically, I comfort myself by …

160. Why is it so hard to eat healthy? I wish …

161. Good health and good sense are two of life's greatest blessings. (Publilius Syrus) I try to use good sense to guide the way I look after my body …

162. I make an effort to stay healthy by …

163. My favorite form of exercise is to …

Goals to be charted

164. These are my New Year's Resolutions:

165. I am going to start changing one thing about myself at a time. I think I will start by …

166. Is it so crazy that I want to be a millionaire by the time I'm …?

167. In order to set goals, you have to have some idea of what you really want. And that's my problem because …

168. Every day I am going to do one kind act. I will start by …

169. I am going to bring more people into my life. I will do this by …

170. I'm bored with just about everything these days. I think I will have to make a goal to go out and do something completely different tomorrow …

171. I am going to stop living in such a state of clutter. My room is …

172. If I could go to any country, I would visit …

173. If I could speak another language, it would be …

174. I am going to save at least half of what I make for the rest of the year so I can …

175. I want a car and this is how I am going to get it:

176. I would like to get my own apartment because …

177. I have some goals for the next season. They include …

#People in my life

178. We must find time to stop and thank the people who make a difference in our lives. (John F. Kennedy) Write a thank-you letter in your journal to someone who has really helped you in your life.

179. My favorite aunt is … because …

180. My cousin ….is interesting because …

181. Of all my teachers, I like …

182. Sometimes people can really disappoint me. Today, for example, I …

183. I don't understand why people can't be kinder to each other. What would happen if …

184. I find it very interesting to meet new people because …

185. I have been wondering if famous people feel any differently about things than ordinary people. Is it possible that …

186. These are the three people who inspire me the most…

187. My grandmother was …

188. The best thing about my mother is …

189. My father is an interesting man. He …

190. The people in my neighborhood are …

191. If I could have a date with anyone I wanted, I would pick … because …

192. Sometimes I wonder where I fit in the lives of the people I know. Do I …

Classes/work

193. My favorite professor is …

194. I think I am half in love with my teacher/boss …

195. My favorite class is …

196. I don't mind studying, but it is hard for me if I can't see that the subject has any relevance in my life. Take … for example. It is …

197. The most frustrating thing about work is …

198. The only class I am always sorry to see the end of is …

199. A funny thing happened in class/work today. We had started …

200. Of all the things I am studying now, is there anything I will remember? I might think sometimes about …

201. Every class has the same kinds of students, and only the names change. There is always a ...

202. My homework/work load is overpowering me. Perhaps I could ...

203. The guy/girl who sits across from me in class is ...

204. How much can we really know another? I know these things about my friend:

205. I think I could go through the rest of my life without ever eating in a cafeteria again because ...

206. There's always something exciting to me about starting a new class/job. I like the ...

#REALLY upset about this

207. My friend promised me we would go somewhere and now they tell me that they have something else to do. I feel like ...

208. I can't believe my best friend would date my boyfriend after we broke up ...

209. Honest disagreement is often a good sign of progress. (Mahatma Gandhi) Is there any way I can turn my fight with ... into a positive learning experience?

210. I've just found out someone I know was saying bad things about me ... I would like to tell them ...

211. Here are my tricks for making my food go farther:

212. I didn't get the promotion and it went to … I am so frustrated because …

213. What kind of a person breaks up with you by sending you a text? Honestly, I can't believe that …

214. There was a mass shooting today on the news…. I believe people do this because ….

215. Sometimes I wonder why I try so hard. I just finished …

216. Why does my life have to be so complicated? Just when I thought I had everything worked out …

217. Sometimes we have to hit bottom before we figure out how to really enjoy life. (Michael Palmer, Miracle Cure) I am really, really upset. I feel like I am at the bottom? This is how it feels … This is what the first rung of the ladder back up looks like …

#Living each day to the fullest

218. Today I just felt so grateful to be alive. I started the day by …

219. Begin at once to live, and count each separate day as a separate life. (Seneca) To be a complete experience, each day for me must contain …

220. Always stay in your own movie. (Ken Kesey) As long as I live my life story on my terms, I feel happy and I am enjoying myself. That means I …

221. I think I am one of the lucky few in this world who gets to live out their dream. I am …

222. Life loves the liver of it. (Maya Angelou) This season, I am re-solving to live each day completely, to know that even though I am young, I need to be conscious of my time. This is how I plan to do this …

223. If you want to be happy, be. (Henry David Thoreau) Can be-ing happy be as easy as making the decision to be it? I will try …

224. May you live all the days of your life. (Jonathan Swift) I love to just goof off because …

225. These are the things that make me happy:

226. The world is so full of a number of things, I'm sure we should all be as happy as kings. (Robert Louis Stevenson) These are the things I want to explore in this world …

227. Strange to say it, but a highlight of my day is walking my dog. We start …

228. People talk about an "authentic" life and I find it hard to pic-ture what that is. I imagine that …

229. Why must we always be doing something to be happy? I remember feeling happy as a child when I was doing nothing, just …

230. I wish there was a step-by-step guide to being happy because it would be a bestseller. My idea of happiness is …

231. My life is really enriched by the joy of having a great group of friends. I don't feel alone because …

Failure and trying again

232. We all make mistakes. The trick is not to let our mistakes make us. Face the music, give thanks for the orchestra and change the tune. (Anonymous) My most crushing failure was when … and this is how I got back on track. I …

233. I don't know which is worse about failing: the disappointment or the humiliation. Today I feel both because …

234. Learn from yesterday, live for today, hope for tomorrow. The important thing is not to stop questioning. (Albert Einstein) I am curious about a lot of things, but often I start things and don't finish them. That is because …

235. Is it possible that we are not meant to complete everything that we try? I wonder because …

236. Perhaps the project was just too enormous, but it seemed doomed to fail from the start. I began feeling that way when …

237. People always say figuratively to get back on the horse that threw you, but I see no need to go through that hurt and humiliation again. Instead I plan to …

238. Failure is supposed to help you grow stronger, but I have failed and all I feel is like a quivering bowl of jelly. I want to …

239. To lose confidence before you start a task is rough, and it can happen to anyone. Sometimes when I get an idea I start to feel …

240. I find it very difficult to accept change. I fight change because I'm afraid of …

#Television takes

241. I'd like to live the way people do in sitcoms because …

242. My favorite television show is …. I like it because …

243. The best actor on television these days is … because …

244. I wonder why television stars make more money than doctors. Could it be that …

245. Whenever I watch … I become disappointed with my own life. I think that I …

246. I cannot watch horror shows because …

247. Watching sports on television is fun, but it's never as much fun as being there in the crowd and experiencing the …

248. My guilty pleasures are … because …

249. The shows that remind me most of my childhood are … because

250. I'm a fan/not a fan of reality TV shows because …

251. The show that best describes my family is …

252. If I could live out the rest of my life in any TV show or movie it would be … because …

253. I always cry when I watch … because it reminds me of …

254. I enjoy the … genre of movie best. These aspects of my personality make me relate most to this kind of movie because …

#My Parents

255. Of all the things my mother/father does for me, the thing I like most is …

256. I don't like how my mother/father acts when …

257. I wish my mother/father would stop being so overprotective/disengaged. I think s/he is like this because …

258. I hate it when my parents fight. It makes me feel …

259. My mom's/dad's best qualities are …

260. Which traits did I inherit most from my parents? Which traits do I like? Are there any traits I wish I didn't have?

261. I wish my mom/dad didn't have to be away so much. If they were around more I would like to …

262. How do I think my parents' childhoods affected their personality today?

263. How do I think my parents' childhoods affected the how they parent today? Did their childhoods positively or negatively affect their parenting styles?

264. How old do you have to be for parents to let you make your own decisions? Should they have a say no matter old you are? Why or why not?

265. Sometimes I feel like I can't stand my parents because …

266. I've never met my real mother/father, and it makes me feel …

267. Since my parents divorced I've felt like …

268. My parents always wanted me to be a … I wish they would understand that …

269. If my parents ever found out I … they would be surprised because …

#Siblings

270. The things I like most about my sibling(s) are …

271. My sibling(s) drive me crazy when …

272. The nicest thing my sibling(s) did for me was …

273. The meanest thing my sibling(s) did to me was …

274. If my sibling(s) ever knew I did … they would feel …

275. How has the birth order of my family affected my personality? How has this birth order affected my sibling(s)?

276. The best/worst things about being the oldest child are?

277. The best/worst things about being the middle child are?

278. The best/worst things about being the youngest child are?

279. I disagree most with my sibling(s) when …

280. My favorite family holiday was when we …

#Future Goals?

281. I wish I had been born with a small compass leading me to my future, because right now I feel quite lost. Perhaps I …

282. An aim in life is the only fortune worth finding. (Robert Louis Stevenson) If my life was ending now, what would I want to be remembered for? Could that be my aim in life?

283. Is it possible to live your whole life without knowing what you want to be? That's how I feel sometimes …

284. Sometimes I like to turn down the noise in my life and dream of what I will become. I think that …

285. The future belongs to those who believe in the beauty of their dreams. (Eleanor Roosevelt) If my life turns out to be perfect, this is how it will look in 10 years …

286. Everything that is done in the world is done by hope. (Martin Luther) Right now I am having doubts that I can become what I want to be, but I keep hoping it will get better soon. I want to …

287. When I dream, I see myself doing …

288. The universe is exactly the size that your soul can encompass. Some people live in extremely small worlds, and some live in a world of infinite possibility. (Kevin Hearne) I am going to live in a big world. This is how it's going to look:

289. If I could pick any job and didn't have to worry about my salary, I would do …

290. Life is a series of natural and spontaneous changes. Don't resist them – that only creates sorrow…Let things flow naturally forward in whatever way they like. (Lao Tzu) If you had told me a few years ago that I would enjoy …, I would have said no way. But I love it because …

291. Lately I've been thinking I might like to be …

292. Don't aim for success if you want it; just do what you love and believe in it, and it will come naturally. (David Frost) There's only one thing I love to do that doesn't even feel like work and that is …

293. There's only one time when my mind feels at ease, and that is when …

294. I'm not sure if it ever works to build a big plan for your life. So many people tell me they stumbled into something they like by accident. What if …

295. Whatever I end up doing in life, I hope it does not involve doing the same thing every day. I want to …

296. The career that would make me the most happy would utilize my strengths in …

297. I know for sure that if I have to… I will not be happy in that career.

298. I want to invent something that will change the world. Perhaps it will …

299. If I study hard and get through college, what I am looking forward to most when I'm done is …

300. Whatever career I end up in, I hope it includes …

#Shopping till we drop

301. Thank God, we're living in a country where the sky's the limit, the stores are open late and you can shop in bed thanks to television. (Joan Rivers) I really enjoy shopping because …

302. It has occurred to me that I might have too much stuff. But when I go shopping, I see things that …

303. In my dreams I can go shopping and buy anything I want. I would …

304. If I won the lottery tomorrow, I would spend my money on the following:

305. The price of anything is the amount of life you exchange for it. (Henry David Thoreau) What do I really want that is worth working extra hours to buy? I guess it would be …

Divorce and its aftermath

306. My parents are getting a divorce and it feels like it might be my fault. I heard …

307. My friend's parents just split and I want to comfort her but I hardly know what to say. I'll tell her that …

308. Some people are just not meant to live together. I think my parents are two of them …

309. Some of my friends haven't even had a real steady relationship yet and here I am getting a divorce. I …

310. Is there anything good that can happen for kids when their parents divorce? Could it …

311. I guess it's time to accept that my mom and dad are just not going to get back together again. I am …

312. The hardest part of my parents' divorce was when they both started to date again. I couldn't …

313. Getting used to the person your parent remarries is one thing, but letting stepbrothers and sisters into your life is harder still. It feels weird because …

314. Nothing has been the same since my parents divorced. I am …

#Death and illness

315. The highest tribute to the dead is not grief but gratitude. (Thornton Wilder) My grandfather/grandmother has just died. Here are five wonderful things he/she taught me about life:

316. Going to a funeral for a loved one gives some a sense of closure. My experience has been ...

317. Why does one person die and another live, even though both were in a horrible accident? Are life's events pre-destined or do we have control over what happens to us? I believe ...

318. Someone I know just committed suicide and I cannot calm my mind. I wish I could understand why ...

319. Dream as if you'll live forever. Live as if you'll die today. (James Dean). My friend just died from an illness/accident. It has left me wondering about my own life and when it might suddenly be taken from me ...

320. If I could bring one dead person back to life for just a day, it would be ... so I could ...

321. Learning that someone you love is terminally ill is a little like learning that a part of your heart is dying too. You ...

322. If I could have another conversation with one important person that I've lost, I would talk to them about ...

323. If I only had six months to live, my bucket list would include …

324. Grieving is a natural process to help us cope with a loss. I grieve best when I …

#Who am I?

325. Sometimes I look at my face in the mirror and a stranger is staring back at me. How can I really know myself?

326. Enlightenment is like the moon reflected on the water. The moon does not get wet, nor is the water broken. (Dogen). Today I got a glimpse of what it would feel like to be enlightened …

327. It has been a long time since I felt myself totally fascinated by something, but it happened today. I was …

328. Three grand essentials to happiness in this life are something to do, something to love, and something to hope for. (Joseph Addison). What can I do, what can I love and what should I hope for?

329. If I had to describe my own personality in one word, I would say that I am …

330. I am tired of well-meaning people in my life demanding that I should be planning it right down to the last second. I want to …

331. Talent hits a target no one else can hit; Genius hits a target

no one else can see. (Arthur Schopenhauer) People tell me that everyone has special talents, but I am not sure what mine are. I think that they might be …

332. If I rated my self-esteem on a scale from 0-10 with 10 being the highest, I would rate myself the following number: … How does this number positively or negatively affect my everyday life?

333. Think about your inner voice and how you talk to yourself. Are you generally supportive of yourself or very critical? If your inner voice were a real friend you interacted with, would you still be friends with them? Why or why not?

334. Is there one big thing that will make me happy in life? Will it just be finding the love of my life, or is it something greater than even that? I must find …

335. My favorite color is … because …

336. If I could be any animal, I would be a …

337. Someone paid me a really nice compliment recently. I had never really considered that. It makes me wonder what other parts of me might be noteworthy as well …

338. When I take a look at my body in the mirror I feel …

339. I need a lot of alone time in my life. I've been that way since …

340. I often dream about … which I think means that …

341. People who know me would be shocked that I …

342. What three words would my friends use to describe me? Why?

343. I have a place in my life for religion because …

344. Wherever I am, I always get the uneasy feeling that I am missing something somewhere else. I want to …

345. I have settled a lot of my problems by taking a walk and today was no different. I …

346. Sometimes I feel like I am alone on this planet. I seem to think differently from so many other people that …

347. I find it hard to go new places all by myself. If I were stronger in my resolve, I would …

348. I once had a bad experience that I think, on reflection, may actually have been a good one. It happened when …

349. One of the nicest things in my life is that unexpected things happen. Today, for example, I …

#My appearance

350. My best physical feature is …

351. People always compliment me on … but I wish they noticed …

352. The part of me that I am most insecure about is … because …

353. How much do I value my appearance? Do I strike a healthy balance of wanting to look good and being reasonable or am I too preoccupied about what other people will think?

354. My friend has promised to send me back home if I ever show up wearing a …

355. I am happiest when I am wearing … because …

356. Sometimes people judge my appearance because …

357. Being tall/short can be a bother because …

358. I like to dress casually because …

359. My favorite outfit to relax in is …

360. My favorite outfit to dress up in is …

361. When I smile …

362. Being physically fit is important to me because …

363. What aspects of my appearance are most like my mother's? My father's?

364. I wish I looked like …

#Challenges and change

365. I need to find ways to stop being so shy. I want to be able to …

366. The hardest thing I have to do is …

367. When I lose my calm, I restore it by ...

368. If we never experience the chill of a dark winter, it is very un-likely that we will ever cherish the warmth of a bright sum-mer's day. (Anton St. Maarten) I feel the chill of tough times. In the days ahead, I expect that ...

369. The biggest challenge I see coming at me next year is to ...

370. The biggest challenge I have ever faced is to ...

371. I am determined to get a date with ..., so I have to figure out how to achieve that. I could ...

372. Remember when life's path is steep, to keep your mind even. (Horace) I can't solve anything tonight because I am too upset. When I wake up tomorrow, I will look at the situation again and see if I can think of a plan.

373. I seem to be pretty good at helping my friends deal with chal-lenges. For example, I ...

374. This is what worked for me the last time I thought I couldn't pass a course. I ...

375. The one thing I am most afraid of facing the in the near future is ...

376. Life is not a problem to be solved, but a reality to be experi-enced. (Soren Keirkegaard) Are my problems dominating my life? I don't think so, but ...

377. Will I ever have time just to do nothing? My life is a little too full right now and I …

378. To make myself known in my company, I must …

379. What would I do if my boss was coming on to me? How would I handle the situation?

380. I sometimes worry that …

381. To be more creative in my work I could …

382. I need to find a way to make more money. I could …

383. My strangest dream is that I am …

384. Lately I find myself seeing the dark side of everything and I'm not sure where that is coming from. I must …

#My hobbies

385. I love to play (sport) because …

386. Is hanging out with your friends a hobby? Why or why not?

387. My favorite lyrics in songs usually have to do with …

388. If I had all kinds of money, I'd arrange my life to just go to one concert after another. I'd follow …

389. I have a tendency to collect things. I like …

390. If I could spend my life on a (beach/mountain/farm, etc.) I'd be happy. I would …

391. If I had a choice to volunteer somewhere I would choose … because …

392. Do I consider myself a creative person? If so, where can I apply my creativity the most?

393. I've always wanted to … as a hobby but have been too reluctant because …

394. When I engage in exercise the feelings I like most are …

395. As long as I have my sketchbook, I never feel bored. I can …

396. If I were to create a scrapbook of special events in my life what would this book contain?

397. Before I die, I am going to learn how to … because …

398. A well-spent day brings happy sleep. (Leonardo da Vinci) On days that end with me feeling my best, usually I have spent some time …

#Money and what it buys

399. There is no wealth but life. (John Ruskin) Money, especially a huge amount of it, is important/unimportant in my life plan. I want to …

400. I never have enough money to do the things I want to do. If I had some real wealth I would …

401. Anything that just costs money is cheap. (John Steinbeck) The things that I value most in life that do not cost money are …

402. Does money really buy happiness?

403. I find it difficult to save any money because ...

404. I need to make more money because ...

405. It always upsets me when I see people wasting money because ...

406. What exactly does it mean to "waste money?" Who decides what has value and what doesn't? I wonder if ...

407. As a student I am really good at stretching my money to the limit. I try to ...

408. If I had one million dollars and couldn't spend it on myself, I would ...

409. Would I rather make one hundred thousand dollars a year in a job that I hate or forty thousand dollars a year in a job that I love? Why?

Travel and where it takes you

410. The city I would most like to spend time in is ...

411. To me, the most exotic travel destination would be ...

412. I am filled with wonder when I look at ...

413. Of all the ways to travel, I prefer ...

414. It is said that everyone has a fairytale destination and mine would be ...

415. If I could improve this Earth in some way, I would …

416. My idea of a great adventure would be to …

417. If I could go to three places anywhere in the world in the next three years, they would be …

418. The most unique travel experience I can think of would be to …

419. To have a perfect vacation at home, I would need …

420. The person, living or dead, whom I would most like to travel with is …

421. If I could go to New York, I would …

422. If the day comes when we can visit other planets, I would like to go to …

#Broken hearted

423. Don't cry because it's over, smile because it happened. (Dr. Seuss) I am in the depths of despair right now, because what I thought would be my "forever" love affair has ended. If I could get past the hurt and the grief, what would I remember about this relationship that was good?

424. The first time I was dumped in a relationship I felt …

425. To be disappointed by someone you love makes you feel like …

426. If my heart was broken, I could learn to trust again by …

427. With a broken heart, my world looks like …

428. My opinion on how long it takes a broken heart to mend is that it …

429. My favorite hurtin' song is …

430. When I think of romance, I think of …

431. The most romantic experience I ever had was when …

432. I wonder if I could have been a better lover and if it would have made any difference. I think about the times when …

433. To be cheated on makes you feel …

434. The most beautiful words of love I have ever heard were …

#Drama kings and queens in my life

435. Chaotic people often have chaotic lives, and I think they create that. But if you try and have an inner peace and a positive outlook, I think you attract that. (Imelda Staunton) The drama queens in my life are …

436. When I am caught up in the drama of someone else's life, I try to …

437. I try not to make my problems too dramatic because …

438. Sometimes I feel like my life is lived in a constant state of crisis. I feel like …

439. Special friends are those with whom you can be silent. I think …

440. I am trying hard not to judge people because …

441. Am I exaggerating my problems? I feel like …

442. I could easily turn into a drama queen if I …

443. When I write in my journal, I feel …

#My senses

444. The prettiest thing I have ever seen was …

445. The thing I saw today that astonished me the most was …

446. Sunsets make me feel …

447. When I look at people, I see …

448. Today I overheard something that was meant to be private. I was …

449. When I wake up in the morning I can heard the birds sing and it makes me want to …

450. I love to hear people laugh. Before I know it, I am …

451. The sounds of a city are …

452. Some sounds make me on edge. For example, when …

453. The strangest flavors I combine are …

454. My favorite dishes are …

455. My favorite picnic food is …

456. My "forbidden fruit" would be …

457. My favorite floral fragrance is …

458. Each season is signaled by signs of its arrival. For example …

459. My favorite spice is …

460. A wood fire burning makes me think of …

461. A child's hug can make you feel like …

462. The best feeling on bare feet is …

463. A massage makes me feel …

#The future

464. When I am old, the world will look much different than it does now. I expect that …

465. If I could make one little change that would make my life better, it would be to …

466. I want to be understanding to myself, to understand others. (Katherine Mansfield) Today I will make a change. I will try to listen more and …

467. There must be a better way to go from city to city than a car, bus or train. We could …

468. I wonder what kind of job I will be doing when I retire. Will I be …

469. I wonder on how many streets I will live in my lifetime. I think that …

470. If people live on other planets, what are they like? I think that …

471. If I were a futurist, I would say that the future will be …

472. My insight for the day is …

473. What if I live to be 110? The world then will look like …

474. My house in the future will be …

475. I may get involved in politics next year because …

Miscellaneous

476. I love lighthouses because …

477. When the power goes out in a storm, I …

478. Learning a second language means …

479. I think I will bring more art into my life now and …

480. We put curtains on windows because …

481. Computers have changed our lives by …

482. I would be lost without my smart phone because …

483. Why does time move so fast sometimes and so slow other times? Is it because …

484. I'd love to have my own personal robot so …

485. Some family reunions are fun, but others can be disastrous ...

486. What is it about fireworks that brings us all together? Is it ...

487. Routine tasks like loading the dishwasher should have some element of fun to them. I think I will ...

488. When I am old, I hope that ...

489. My relationship with time is ...

490. I am glad I have not lived through a world war because ...

491. My favorite author is ...

492. I can't leave home without my ...

493. My favorite piece of technology is my ...

494. I wish I didn't know that ...

495. The best present I ever received was ...

496. Where do ideas come from? I think that ...

497. The most useful of all gadgets is the ...

498. What will I be doing five years from now? I think that ...

499. I would like to raise ... children because ...

500. The one book I can read again and again is ...

501. The thing I like most about my bedroom is ...

502. When I cook, the thing I make best is ...

PART THREE

Most journals are kept like traditional diaries. But for the adventurous journal-writer, there are other kinds of journals to capture your thoughts, memories and imagination in different formats.

Here are 25 different ideas and inspirations for creative journaling.

1. Photo journal – Using your digital camera, take one photo each day and save it either in an online photo journal or a printed one. Be sure to add captions and date the photo. If you like, you can pick one particular theme like a hobby or your friends.

2. Card journal – Create a journal to save all your special greeting cards. From your first valentines to congratulations on your first apartment, cards often represent the milestones in your life. If you want to store your cards electronically, just scan them and store them in an online journal

3. Letters journal – Not too many people send letters anymore, but those who do often compose them for special occasions and messages and they are worth saving. Even special letters sent electronically can be saved and printed for inclusion in your letters journal. Save letters you write as well.

4. Quotation journals – Quotations can often sum up the way you feel about something or inspire you. Keep a journal of those special sayings that mean a lot in your life.

5. Relationship journals – Chronicle your romantic relationships by dedicating one relationship at a time, even if you think each one is going to be the one of a lifetime. You will laugh and learn as the years pass, or have fond memories if the relationships go on forever.

6. Couple's journal – Keep a couple's journal where every day each of you writes one thing that you really appreciate about the other person each day.

7. Book journal – Keep a journal of every book that you read and a brief review of what you thought of it and whether or not you felt it was worth reading.

8. Birthday journal – Keep a journal that will last a lifetime, recording all the details of how you celebrate the passing of each year. If you have a party, talk about the theme, the food, and special surprises. If you attend the birthday parties of friends and family members as well, why not include them in your birthday journal as well.

9. Construction journal – If you decide to have your house built, record the progress of the building day by day, all the way through to the final painting of the walls and decorating touches. It will be a wonderful memory of your special home.

10. Map journal – Collect maps from every community and country that you visit and save them in a journal along with three or four bullet points highlighting key memories of the trip.

11. Art journal – Save your sketches and doodles all together in a large-size journal that will be fascinating to chart your progress over the years. Try to add something each week to your art journal.

12. Travel journal – Travel is as much about personal development as it is about seeing the world. At the end of each day, whether you are in an airport, on a cruise ship or settled into a quaint bed and breakfast, give a succinct account of where you are, what you saw and what you think about it. Over a lifetime of travels, you will amass a fascinating collection of impressions.

13. Diet journal – Research has shown that dieters who keep journals about what they eat each day have more success than those who do not. Start by talking about your personal weight goals and why you want to achieve them, and which diet you are selecting. Then record your meals, your impressions and great new recipes.

14. Dream journal – We all dream and sometimes we remember them for a few hours the next morning, and then they are gone. However, it has become quite trendy for people seeking illumination from their dreams to record them and determine if there are trends or dreams that keep recurring.

15. Goal journal – By assembling all your goals in one journal and breaking them down into actual plans, you may be more likely to achieve them. Watch how your goals change over the

years or how many times a variation of the same goal reappears.

16. To-do list journal – If you really want a chronicle of how you spend your days, save your daily to-do lists in a journal. You will be amazed at what you really accomplish and how your priorities change with the seasons and the years.

17. Gratitude journal – Keep a written reminder of something you are grateful for each day. Top it off with special entries about Thanksgiving Day and how you spend it.

18. Concert ticket journal – Ticket stubs from music concerts, ball games, stage productions and art galleries all add up to the story of exciting times in your lives. Keep them all in one journal with a couple of bullet points about highlights of the event and you will always remember the great moments in your life.

19. Essay journal – Think of all the hours you spend creating essays on a wide variety of subjects through high school and university. Save your work in a journal and watch your progress and occasional failures, and enjoy reading them again a few years from now.

20. Selfie journal – Take at least one interesting self a week and watch how your looks and styles change over the course of a year or two.

21. Recipe journal – Start collecting excellent recipes that you encounter from friends and family members and other sources.

If you collect old family recipes, add a short note about who gave it to you and when you enjoyed eating it.

22. Movie journal – In a separate journal, keep a list of all the movies that you see and add a few sentences about whether or not you enjoyed them and your overall impressions.

23. Technology journal – Each time you purchase a new piece of technology, take a picture of it and keep it in your journal along with the receipt, the instruction journal and your impressions of it. In the beginning it will be handy to have things where you might need them; in the long run, you will find it fascinating to see how dramatically technology advances.

24. Friend journal – Dedicate one entire journal to the joys and pleasures of good friendships. Add pictures of every gathering and close-ups of friends that share so many of life's great experiences with you.

25. Wish journal – Wishes fall short of goals but are more realistic than dreams. You can fill a journal with them by doing everything from cutting out something from a catalogue to jotting down a quick note about something you believe would be great to do in the future.

I want to personally thank all of you who purchased this book.

Can I ask you for a favor?

If you found this book helpful I would really appreciate if you could leave a quick review on Amazon for my book. You can go to this link here to leave a review: http://amzn.to/1Mo9nhm

I love hearing from my readers and read all of my reviews. Book reviews are SO important for independent authors like me to help get my work out to a larger audience!

Thanks,

Emilee Day